03-11

TIME TO LEARN ABOUT
PAST, PRESENT
& FUTURE

Pam Scheunemann

Consulting Editor, Diane Craig, M.A./Reading Specialist

Published by ABDO Publishing Company, 8000 West 78th Street, Edina, Minnesota 55439.

Copyright © 2008 by Abdo Consulting Group, Inc. International copyrights reserved in all countries.

No part of this book may be reproduced in any form without written permission from the publisher. SandCastle™ is a trademark and logo of ABDO Publishing Company. Printed in the United States.

Editor: Pam Price
Content Developer: Nancy Tuminelly
Cover and Interior Design and Production: Mighty Media
Photo Credits: BananaStock Ltd., JupiterImages Corporation, ShutterStock

Library of Congress Cataloging-in-Publication Data

Scheunemann, Pam, 1955-
  Time to learn about past, present & future / Pam Scheunemann.
      p. cm. -- (Time)
  ISBN 978-1-60453-017-9
  1. Time--Juvenile literature. I. Title. II. Title: Time to learn about past, present and future.
  QB209.5.S34 2008
  529--dc22

                                     2007030075

time

Time is an interesting thing. You can't touch it. You can't see it. You can't hold it. But it is always passing by!

Let's learn about time in the past, the present, and the future!

time

3

Cindy would like to go outside to play. She wishes she had done her homework yesterday. Yesterday is the day before today. Yesterday is in the past.

past

The past means all the time before right now.

time fact

Telephones were invented a long time ago. Telephones have changed over time. Telephones looked different in the past.

Things that happened a long time ago are in the past.

time
fact

Dinosaurs lived a very, very long time ago. Dinosaurs are extinct. Ted's family imagines what they were like by looking at their bones. This one sure was big!

Dinosaurs lived more than 65 million years ago.

time fact

present

The present is right now.
You are reading this sentence
in this book in the present.
The page you just read is
already in the past.

The present is the moment that is right now.

time fact

The moment you taste the cool, sweet flavor of an ice-cream cone happens in the present. Ed's favorite flavor is vanilla. If you are thinking about how much you enjoyed an ice-cream cone before, you are thinking about the past.

The first ice-cream parlor opened in 1776 in New York City. That was more than 200 years in the past.

time fact

present

Mara loves her cat Whiskers. When she pets him and hears his purring, that is in the present. Sometimes Mara thinks about when he was a kitten. Then she is remembering the past.

Abraham Lincoln had cats in the White House when he was president. That was in the past.

time fact

Laurie likes to watch plants grow. She is holding the plant now. When she plants it and gives it sun and water, it will grow. Laurie is planning for the future.

A redwood tree can live more than 1,000 years. If you plant one now, it will not be fully grown until far into the future.

time fact

16

future

Michael loves to draw. He is showing his artwork now. He learned about drawing in the past year. Michael hopes to go to art school in the future.

time fact

Artists often use sketchbooks to draw their ideas. They use their ideas to plan future works.

future

Emma is shorter than her older sister. In a few years, Emma will be taller than she is at the present time. In the future, she may even grow taller than her sister.

time fact

No one really knows the future. We do know that all things change over time.

past

present

future

One way to think about time is in terms of past, present, and future.

Yesterday is in the past. Today is in the present. Tomorrow is in the future.

Things we have already done are in the past.
Things we do right now are in the present.
Things we will do are in the future.

time fact

Do you remember a favorite time in your past?

What are you doing right now?

What do you want to do in the future?

23

Glossary

imagine – to make a picture of something in your mind.

invention – a new thing that is created because someone had the idea to make it. Cars, glasses, and soap were all invented by people.

parlor – a place of business, such as an ice-cream parlor or a beauty parlor.

sentence – a group of words that includes a subject and a verb.

sketchbook – a book or a pad of paper used for drawing sketches.

White House – the official home of the president of the United States.

To see a complete list of SandCastle™ books and other nonfiction titles from ABDO Publishing Company, visit **www.abdopublishing.com**.
8000 West 78th Street, Edina, MN 55439
800-800-1312 • 952-831-1632 fax